Reflections from the Valley Floor

David L. Bateman

WHAT OTHERS ARE SAYING

"Pastor David is one of the Lord's Mighty Men who has endured the storms of life and is still standing and fighting strong… his words of encouragement will bring life to any struggling or weary warrior." - Pastor Michael Morris; Pastor of Pastoral Care; Seacoast Church

"David has taken his valley experiences and expressed them in ways in which we can all identify. He shows us that it is okay to ask the hard questions as we go through our own valleys of pain. David does an excellent job of relating examples in Scripture to the difficulties we face, which gives us the confidence to get up from the valley floor and stand triumphantly with Jesus!" - Faye S. Hill, President, Lowcountry Pregnancy Center

"These devotional thoughts will encourage you in your darkness and pain. You will be inspired to keep going and keep trusting God. David Bateman speaks with compassion and experience. He shows all of us that God is still there when things are tough." - Pastor Ron Dillon, First Baptist Church, Mount Pleasant

"Wisdom, truth, practical, challenging, convicting, encouraging, hopeful: these are but a few of the words that describe this 30 day journey David Bateman has put together for those enduring pain and suffering. I heartily commend it to you." - Chaplain (Major) Erik J. Gramling – U.S. Army Chaplain

"David is a rare man of God that is actually doing the hard work of shepherding people's souls. Genuine, deep, terrifying, and hopeful - time spent in this book is a privilege that will bring strength to the frail and light in the valley." – Pastor Jeff Miller, Vineyard Community Church, Augusta

Hospitals are our last monasteries, filled with folk suffering from illnesses and or traumatic events. For those hospitalized or at home, David Bateman's book is a healing guide for reflection upon scriptural truths and the presence of God in one's pain and suffering. - Terry Wilson, Chaplain, Medical University of South Carolina

"People are now realizing that it's the valley experiences that give them hope, so be not afraid. In the midst of the storm, GOD is always near. David, thanks for encouraging us, and helping us to understand that life is a process. If we just endure…what great reward awaits us. You are truly an inspiration to all. - Sharon Taylor, RN, Beacon Hospice Director

"As Bateman wrestles with God in "the valley of the shadow," he enables us to struggle with what Pascal called the dignity and misery of our human journey. As we venture through life's "dangers, toils and snares," Bateman feeds us with life-giving pastoral care and extraordinarily relevant biblical wisdom." - Dean K. Thompson - President and Professor of Ministry Emeritus, Louisville Presbyterian Theological Seminary

"I commend to you David's devotional book, *Reflections from the Valley Floor*. You will find in it a richness and depth meant to help you grow as a Christian. As with a person of David Bateman's character and temperament, it is written not as much "to," and hardly "at" you, as it is written "with" you, in the way we as Christians are called to bear one another's burdens and share each others' joy (I Corinthians 12: 26)." - The Reverend Robert M. Knight, D. Min. Charleston (SC) Pastoral Counselor

"Reflections from the Valley Floor presents theological truths with clarity and helpful illustrations from an experienced minister. The format provides an opportunity to reflect upon the devotional and this is an ideal resource for anyone going through a challenging time. Thank you David for giving perspective to those who are in a valley." – Rick Higgins, Associate Pastor, The Church at LifePark

"David Bateman is a colleague, a brother in Christ, and a friend. His miles of experience on the road of life entitle him to write to as a "fellow pilgrim." His words on these pages will definitely reach into your soul and promote liberating thought as you glean from his reflections on life-lessons graced by the mercies of the Lord Jesus." - Tim Hodge, Lead Pastor, Crossroads World Outreach Center.

DEDICATION

To my children,

David Stephen
Sarah Leanne
Shanleigh Ruth
Summer Grace
Serena Ruth

Besides the Lord and your mom, you are my greatest delights.
I am very proud of you and excited to see what God has in
store for you. You will, no doubt, face seasons on the valley
floor. I pray that this little book will remind you of the
enduring perfect love of your Abba Father and the devoted
(yet imperfect) love of your dad.

ACKNOWLEDGMENTS

My wife, Laurie, we have shared many joys on the
mountaintop and many tears in the valley. I'm glad we've done
it together and you never let go of my hand.

My parents, Larry and Jane Bateman, you have taught and
displayed so much about perseverance
producing character and hope. Thank you.

My sister, Rebekah Clough, I am glad that we share more than
just a painful past. I'm proud of you.

My brother, Daniel, [1968-1992], you would have done a much
better job of writing this book, but you taught me about love,
disappointment, and hanging in there.

My house church family, you all supported, prayed, and loved
me through my last journey in the valley floor.

My CPE supervisors, Helen Waugh and Bill Swinton, along
with the Roper St. Francis CPE interns, residents, and staff,
you helped me learn so much more about love, ministry,
awareness, and mystery.

My ministry colleagues, you invited me to grow to live within
the tension of the "here and not yet"

My editors, Sara Richmond and Caroline Clayton, your one-
two punch was perfect for this.

CONTENTS

Forward from a Fellow Pilgrim

I write as a fellow pilgrim. I have my own stories of sorrow and joy, of pain and wholeness, and you have yours too. Though each journey is unique, we face many of the same questions and hardships. My granddad died at 84; my brother died at 24 - I miss them both. My wife recently faced major cancer surgery. If you've lived any length of time you know the warmth of sunlight on the mountaintop and you've navigated the shadows in the valley floor.

I've seen that we all spend some time in the valley. I recall the lady who was about to check out of the hospital who needed to call a taxi for a ride; no one else was around. I sat with families as loved ones slipped into eternity in the midst of our prayers. I found many old ladies who were tired of treading the valley floor, but still spread a hope that could come only from God. As a fellow pilgrim who has been able to walk through the valley with others, I offer some daily reflections for your own journey. My goal is not so we see all things clearly, but we encounter the One who is the Light and in Him there is no darkness at all. I really believe that the Divine flows through the valley as much as on the mountain.

Each day has a reflection and then space for your own stories, images, and echoes. I hope you will use this booklet as a tool in your own journey. My prayer is that God will bring us to a place where we are joyfully surprised by his power and love, regardless of circumstances.

God's peace to you.

-David Bateman, Charleston, South Carolina

1. Is it Alright to Wrestle with Faith and God?

It isn't that we don't believe in God anymore, it's that we feel confused, hurt, and disillusioned. We prayed, we believed, and it doesn't seem like it made any difference at all. We find ourselves in a civil war. We may love God and believe in God, but we're angry with God. We have lots of questions. Do you ever feel this way? When I do, I sometimes feel guilty because religion tells people of faith not to feel this way, right? Let's think about that for a moment.

Imagine that God is giving you permission to wrestle and struggle with your faith and your feelings. He is okay with your angst. The struggle is not against your faith; the struggle is within your faith. It is part of faith. The civil war in our emotions and beliefs may actually strengthen our faith. God can handle the questions and the cussing. Our tears and our anger touch him. It is okay that what we *know* fights against how we *feel*. You will never find a Scripture of God blasting someone for being honest about feelings. God never heaps guilt on a person for not bottling up disappointment. Some of God's closest friends were quite expressive about the depths of their pain. It has taken me a long time to learn to be vulnerable with the Lord, but it has been worth it!

The most famous Psalm is Psalm 23. I've heard Psalm 23 numerous times. "The Lord is my shepherd...quiet waters...restores my soul...valley of the shadow of death...You are with me." It is a wonderful and very inspirational Psalm. David, as a former shepherd, saw God as His Shepherd. We hallmark David's faith in the Lord as the ideal, but David didn't get to Psalm 23 faith until he went through Psalm 22 faith. Take a look at Psalm 22. His lament to God shows the conflict of faith. "My God, My God, why have you forsaken me...You do not answer...I find no rest." David's pain does not end with a period, but with a comma. "I find no rest, yet You are enthroned as the Holy One...but I am a worm...all who see me mock me...yet You brought me out of the womb." David deeply expressed his feelings, but he did so against the backdrop of what he knew for sure. David, a man after God's own heart, did not bury his disappointment or apologize for his feelings. He didn't sit in his sorrow. He was brutally honest with God. David shows us we can say anything to God. It is okay for us to verbalize our pain. Amazingly, Jesus quoted David's Psalm 22, not Psalm 23, in his darkest moments on earth and you can too. Now what do you want to say to God?

My Reflections

_____

_____

_____

_____

_____

_____

_____

_____

_____

_____

2. Touched by the Feelings of Our Weaknesses

A politician once said, "I feel your pain" and my response was, "Really?" Don't you hate it when people say, "Oh, I know how you feel!" even when they don't have a clue? One of my favorite promises is Psalm 34: "The LORD is close to the brokenhearted and saves those who are crushed in spirit." The Lord is near when we no longer feel in control or when our lives are shattered. The Psalmist used a powerful word for close: "God is close enough to touch." Let's realize that the Lord helps those who canNOT help themselves.

My grandfather served stateside in the Navy during World War 2. He and his wife had a little baby. He was driving hours a day for duty. Time was precious; money was tight. Alcohol became his friend. Granddad was trying to cope with life, but alcohol betrayed him and drew him into addiction. One particular night of wrestling with the demons of his soul he cried out to God from the kitchen floor, "God help me because I cannot help myself." That night was a turning point for granddad. God was near to him in his pain and anxiety and created space in his heart for healing to come.

As a Christian I love the promise that the Lord is touched by the feelings of our weaknesses (Hebrews 4.15). He knows and really understands pain, rejection and feelings of fear. He loves us to tell Him about how we feel, and in his understanding, is able to tailor his grace to meet our deepest need. We don't have to fix ourselves before we come to the compassionate God. The old song, "Just As I Am" comes to mind. I'm no longer embarrassed to bring my fears and doubts and hurts. God is truly able to say, "I feel your pain."

My Reflections

_____

_____

_____

_____

_____

_____

_____

_____

_____

_____

_____

_____

_____

_____

_____

_____

_____

_____

_____

_____

3. I Will Not Waste This Pain

A little girl whose name isn't even given in the Bible holds a special place in my heart. You can read about her in 2 Kings 5, but here's the gist of the story: a little Israelite girl was kidnapped from her family and sold as a maid slave to a Syrian general and his wife. Can you imagine the trauma and pain that this little girl experienced? How she missed her family? Where was God in all this? She had every reason to hate her captors and wish for their demise.

One day she found out that her master, the Syrian general, had leprosy. If I were in her sandals, I would have been jumping for joy! "Serves him right, now God is getting him back!" "I hope he rots away…" She actually does the exact opposite, she tells him about the One True God of Israel and His prophet, Elisha. The general actually ends up going to Israel, meeting the prophet, and being healed of his disease. He turns from his own gods to become a follower of the God of Israel.

What I love about this story is how this little girl teaches me not to waste my pain. Painful memories of my brother's accident, my loss of friends, and my loneliness still leave a bitter taste in my mouth, but the little girl inspires me from her pain. She was hurt and deeply traumatized. She was in a strange land as a slave. She could no longer run and play with her friends. She could no longer sit on her mama's lap before going to sleep. She could have become so absorbed with her story and stifled by her loss that she would have missed her calling. The grace of God met her in her pain and enabled her to share the love of God with another who was also hurting.

May God give us the grace not only to endure, but also to

never waste our pain. May He leverage our pain and story so others are touched by the overflowing love and power of God.

My Reflections

_____

_____

_____

_____

_____

_____

_____

_____

_____

_____

_____

_____

_____

_____

_____

_____

_____

4. The Mystery of Why

Inquisitive minds want to know. I remember my kids' curiosity going off the chart. Why is the sky blue? Why are my eyes brown? Why is wind so windy? On and on it goes. Age and experience don't stop the desire to know, do they? Even in the midst of pain, suffering, or disappointment, we want to know why. We want to understand all that is happening or could happen. And we wonder why.

God invites us to ask why.

You'll recall in Matthew 27.46 that from the cross, Jesus even asked God, "My God, my God, why have you forsaken me?" I'm sure plenty of people could have given Jesus all "the" reasons. Religious people love to explain what they think.

In the midst of our "why" questions and everyone's pat answers is the mystery of our moment. We may need to ask why like Jesus did, and we may find an answer, but sometimes the answer does not come this side of heaven. I still have questions of why cancer cells were found and why the grouchy person felt led to attend church with me. Why was the other person picked for the job? Embracing the mystery has become part of my journey through the valley. I desire answers, but have to let go of my demand for answers. There are some things that we simply can't explain well, though we try.

I'm brought into the mystery of God's love and power in Acts chapter 12. Peter is in jail and scheduled for execution, but God sends an angel who opens the jail doors and takes Peter to freedom. There is just one problem for me. The story begins with, *"It was about this time that King Herod arrested some who belonged to the church, intending to persecute them. He had James, the brother of John, put to death with the sword."* I sure am glad for Peter's miracle, but what about James? I begin to ask, "God, couldn't You have...?" and there I am again embracing the mystery of why. And sometimes, we just don't know. Let's keep asking why. Sometimes we'll get an answer and sometimes we won't. Regardless, we will choose to trust the God of the mystery.

My Reflections

_____

_____

_____

_____

_____

_____

_____

_____

_____

_____

_____

_____

_____

_____

5. Some Things Only Make Sense in Reverse

Trusting feels a lot easier when things begin to make sense. There are times when we can look back and see that God was up to something behind the scenes, way bigger than we could imagine. Other times we wonder what is going on. Is God doing anything? How could He be? God feels a million miles away. So when you look at things, sometimes they don't make any sense at all.

You may recall the biblical story of Joseph, in Genesis 37-50. Joseph was the younger brother of Jacob's ten sons. When all the sons were out of town, they took Joseph, threw him in a pit, and then sold him into slavery. Joseph's faith sustained him and God blessed him in the midst of much pain and loss. Over and over, Joseph did the right thing. He even had a chance to sleep with a seductive woman, and he said, "No!" What was Joseph's reward for doing the right thing? He was falsely accused of attempted rape and thrown into prison. Now if I were Joseph I would wonder, "What did I do to deserve this? I've done the right thing and what is my reward? How could God let me go through this? Is there any end?"

As the story progresses, Joseph stayed with God and even served his fellow man. What reward did he receive? A man he helped, who held the key to his release, forgot him for 3 years! When all looked hopeless, God raised Joseph up from the prison to the palace. Joseph is placed as God's go-between for the people who faced severe famine and possible death. When Joseph had the opportunity to be reunited with his brothers who betrayed him, he stated, "You intended to harm me, but God intended it for good to accomplish what is now being done, the saving of many lives." (Genesis 50.20)

Joseph had an "aha" moment. He could look and see that God was up to something. God didn't waste Joseph's pain and loss. He redeemed it for good. You may look at your situation today and wonder, "How could God bring anything good out of my story?" The answer is, "I don't know; it would take a God-sized miracle, for sure." Sometimes we have the "aha" moment, like Joseph, and see what God is doing in the midst of pain. Others times we have no clue. You may want to tell the Lord that you want Him to bring good out of your pain. Tell Him you will keep trusting Him even if it doesn't make sense until we reach the other side.

My Reflections

_____

_____

_____

_____

_____

_____

_____

_____

_____

_____

_____

_____

6. God Didn't Do What I Thought He Would

Many faithful people who knew God and the Scriptures well were still amazed and deeply saddened at how Jesus' life on earth seemed to end. The One who had said and done so much was tortured on a cross? How were they to know that the coming of the King and the fullness of the Kingdom would not be in the same season of history? They, as we, didn't fully understand God's timing or His ways. If I had lived during the Roman times, or the Nazi times, for that matter, I would have been so sure that I knew what God was going to do next.

The trouble is, God doesn't always do what I think He should. Just recently I was a finalist for a job that seemed like the perfect fit. I prayed on it and I sensed that God said, "You will get the job, but it won't be easy; it will be stretching." I actually did not get the job. God didn't do what I thought He would and I was really disappointed.

Years ago after my brother Daniel's head injury, we were sure God would heal him on my dad's birthday. Then we were sure it would be Thanksgiving, then Christmas, then New Years, and then we were no longer sure. It wasn't until 17 years later that Daniel went to heaven and received his complete healing.

Many disillusioned pilgrims have given up on the valley floor. I have to keep remembering that God works off of *His* vast plan and calendar while I watch *my* clock. He is not in as much of a hurry as I am. God promised Abraham (age 75) that he would become a great nation with many descendants. God began fulfilling that promise 25 years later. God did what He said He would, just not in the timing or way others assumed.

My Reflections

_____

_____

_____

_____

_____

_____

_____

_____

_____

_____

_____

_____

_____

_____

_____

_____

_____

_____

_____

_____

_____

7. Waking Me Up This Mo'nin'

While in college I had a ministry assignment at a church on the south side of Chicago. Every week the Sunday School director, a godly grey-haired lady, would gather us all in a circle. She always wore a white dress with matching gloves.

She made all the kids and volunteers hold hands and would lead us in a prayer. A strong voice, echoing from her 4'10" frame, commanded our attention.

She would always start her prayer the same way, "Lord, thank you for waking us up this mo'nin'; thank you for giving us a day that wasn't promised to us."

As an 18 year old, I thought her prayer was silly. I had never heard anyone pray that way before. As I've grown I have realized how true her prayer is. Every day is a gift from the Lord. It wasn't promised to us. The Lord woke us up this morning, even when we thought it was the alarm clock.

"Lord, thank you for waking me up this morning. Thank you for the gift of life. Please help me experience life to the fullest. I don't want to miss out on whatever you have for me, in this life or the next." Amen.

My Reflections

_____

_____

_____

_____

_____

_____

_____

_____

_____

_____

_____

_____

_____

_____

_____

_____

_____

_____

_____

_____

_____

_____

8. Honest to God

Many good people of faith have a hard time offering intense honesty to God and themselves. Whether the TV preacher, the neighbor down the street, or the friend from church, we are often encouraged to just say positive words of faith. "Claim it!" "Speak only words that affirm and build up!" It can become like a spiritualized superstition or a religious jinx.

Sadly, many will exclaim, "If you verbalize the hurt you feel then you are not walking in faith!" I imagine that God would challenge this idea. Consider these words of pain lived out in the heart of faith. Jesus said, "My soul is overwhelmed with sorrow to the point of death." St. Paul said, "We were under great pressure, far beyond our ability to endure, so that we despaired of life itself." That doesn't sound very saintly does it? Job cried, "know that God has wronged me and drawn his net around me. "Though I cry, 'Violence!' I get no response; though I call for help, there is no justice."

Just as Job, Paul and even Jesus expressed brutal feelings to God. What is it that you want to say to God? Let us be honest about what is going on in our hearts, even when we do not understand it or even like it. I recall walking through the hallways of our church building screaming at God as loud as I could. He heard me and got me through a very dark time.

You may write a letter to God. You don't have to show it to anyone, but you might want to show it to God. You will walk in fine company with people who have poured out their deepest hearts before the Lord. God can, still, handle it and bring you through. Faith is lived out deeply in the midst of being honest to God.

My Letter to God

_____

_____

_____

_____

_____

_____

_____

_____

_____

_____

_____

_____

_____

_____

_____

_____

_____

_____

_____

_____

9. Why Do I Want God to Show Up?

The more we realize that God is active and not passive, the more we invite him into all the nitty gritty of life. I often pray with sick persons and ask God to show up in their lives and situations. So when we pray for God to show up in our lives, why do we ask? My easy answer is, "I want to be well and feel better." There is certainly nothing wrong with asking God to make me well. Have you ever considered asking God to show up in your situation for reasons that go beyond just yourself? This is not an easy thought, is it?

An amazing story in Isaiah 36-37 shows pleadings and prayers that go beyond quick relief. King Hezekiah asked God to show up when Jerusalem was surrounded and the enemy was closing in. Israel was outnumbered and in dire straits. The people's distress swelled with the taunts and slander of the enemy. They could only imagine how this huge juggernaut could squash them, kill them, and enslave their children.

In the midst of fear, Hezekiah blessed God's power and authority. He honestly shared the plight of his people and their prospects for success, but look at how he finished his prayer: "Now, LORD our God, deliver us from his hand, so that all the kingdoms of the earth may know that you, LORD, are the only God." (Isaiah 37.20) Isn't that amazing? Wouldn't it be great for God to be glorified through your journey on the valley floor?

Keep on asking God to show up and relieve pain and suffering, but ask him to do that and so much more: may people everywhere see the amazing love and power of God.

My Reflections

10. One Day at a Time

The Lord's Prayer in Matthew 6 is very popular. "Thy Kingdom Come" gets a lot of attention. The prayer finishes with a bang, "Thine is the Kingdom and the power and the glory, forever!" Tucked away in the middle is a short phrase easily overlooked. Can you guess which phrase seems to hide? In the middle is a little prayer: "Give us today our daily bread." I used to think that statement was just about lunch. Now I see that it covers so much more than food. The prayer helps me say, "Lord, give me **today** what I need to handle today."

When I am sick or hurting, my mind easily races ahead to the future. I continually replay a lot of "What ifs?" I am sick. What if I get sicker? What if I can't work? What if I can't pay my bills? Who will take care of my dog? Will my kids be able to finish school? Who will take care of the family? Who will mow the yard? What will happen to my spouse? My mind races faster and faster. It is in those times that the Lord brings up the little prayer, "Give us today our daily bread."

I rarely see God give me tomorrow's bread, today. Normally, I see God give **today** the grace or strength or hope that is needed for **today**. When Moses was leading the Israelite people from captivity to the Promised Land, the Lord provided daily bread called, "manna" from heaven. It was God's daily provision for his people to make it one more day. I've seen God's daily grace get me through teething babies, job struggles, marriage trials, and financial uncertainty. His daily bread is the portion that satisfies. What do you need for today? Why not offer a prayer, "God, I am hurting. Please give me **today** what I need to handle today."

My Reflections

11. The Best Day and the Worst Day

As a Christian, I look at the *worst* event in human history as the crucifixion of Jesus Christ, the sinless Son of God. The greatest travesty of injustice was committed the day He died. As a Christian, I look at the *best* event in human history as the crucifixion of Jesus Christ, the sinless Son of God. The greatest act of love was shown the day He died.

How can this be? How could the worst and best day be the same day? It was very bad, wasn't it? Yes, the religious leaders were in cahoots with lots of evil people to mock, beat, torture and then kill the Author of Life! God knew that the rebellion and selfishness of humanity must be punished and He lovingly sent His Son to take the punishment for you and me. The Scripture teaches that when I turn from going my own way and put my trust and dependence in what Jesus did and is now doing, I am adopted into God's family, my sin is cleaned up, I am declared not guilty, and I am filled with His Presence (Ephesians 2:1-10).

I tell you that for two reasons: 1) because God loves you deeply and wants you to experience His love and forgiveness too. If you haven't had a conversation inviting Jesus to be your leader and forgiver, today is a great day – He is listening. If that feels too heavy, maybe you can just tell Jesus, "I'm going to start saying `yes' to You." (2) I also tell you that because God is able to pull it off. God is able to use the worst day ever to make the greatest day ever. You may be feeling that there is no good purpose that God could ever bring out of the suffering that you are experiencing. We have to keep the cross as the backdrop of suffering and pain. If God can pull it off for Jesus, He can pull it off for you.

My Reflections

_____

_____

_____

_____

_____

_____

_____

_____

_____

_____

_____

_____

_____

_____

_____

_____

_____

_____

12. The Power of Silence

This is what the Sovereign LORD, the Holy One of Israel, says:

*"In repentance and rest is your salvation,
in quietness and trust is your strength..." (Isaiah 30.15)*

When we're hurting, we may not have the opportunity to reflect quietly. We may be busy with jobs or appointments or people. We may try to keep a hectic pace, but sometimes there is a yearning for quiet. Your hurt and story are different from every other and there are seasons when we try to process what is going on inside and outside. Sometimes we simply feel all alone, whether we want to or not. Wounds and scars abound but sometimes they are isolating.

I've seen patients who have withdrawn into something like a cave for healing. Their comforter on the bed becomes the comforter for their heart. They just don't have a lot to say. Trying to heal is exhausting. Long conversations bring fatigue.

The silence is actually okay and the quietness brings healing. In the midst of the quiet is a God who loves you. It is nice to be with someone when you don't have to talk. With God, you can just be. He likes being with us, beside the still waters. There is a place with God that is quiet. We stop trying to save ourselves. All we can do is rest in silence. It is not a silence of resignation or defeat; it is a stillness of trust and release... of letting go. Surprisingly, it is in those moments that we find strength - for in the silence He is holding us.

My Reflections

_____

_____

_____

_____

_____

_____

_____

_____

_____

_____

_____

_____

_____

_____

_____

_____

_____

_____

_____

_____

13. Who Am I Really?

If you have prolonged suffering and pain, it is scary when you begin to get used to it. "That is just the way it is" feels like the mantra of life. Stop for a moment and consider: Has your sickness become your new identity? Are you being reduced to a medical label or diagnosis? Wait a moment! You are not sick; you have a sickness. You may battle depression, but that is not who you are. You may spend countless hours in treatment and endless visits to specialists. It may become easy for your waking hours to be so consumed with sickness that you are shocked to consider that it is NOT you! It may be hard to remember being anything but sick. It may feel like all anyone ever talks about is sickness. "How do you feel? Do you need anything? Are you doing better? When is your next appointment? I like the other radiologist better. You can't eat that because it messes with your meds." On and on it goes! Wouldn't it be nice to sometimes talk about football or flowers? You may battle a sickness but it is not who you are. So who are you?

You are a creation of God. You were put together in your mother's womb. You are fearfully and wonderfully made. You are deeply loved by God. He would die rather than have you be apart. God knows the number of hairs on your head. He never forgets you! Doctors may give a diagnosis, but doctors never decide your destiny or identity. How does this promise to the people of God speak to your heart? "The LORD your God is with you, the Mighty Warrior who saves. He will take great delight in you; in his love he will no longer rebuke you, but will rejoice over you with singing." (Zephaniah 3.17)

26

Can you imagine the God of the universe being so delighted in you that He composed a song dedicated to you? You may spend hours finding out what sickness you have, but you may also want to spend time finding out who God says you really are. Who you are lasts, what you have doesn't. Behind all the things that aren't well is a beautiful masterpiece of God. The same God who made the sunset delights over you....because you are.

My Reflections

_____

_____

_____

_____

_____

_____

_____

_____

_____

_____

_____

_____

_____

_____

14. Overcoming The Unseen Enemy

I personally take the story of the fall of humankind at face value. When the first couple chose to eat the fruit, something deeper was going on. More than just a poor pick, their action was declaring to God, "I want to do what I want to do." Since their first choice against God, our world has been filled with pain, sickness, sorrow, and injustice. When we read about war, famine, strife, and corruption, it all goes back to the choice of our first parents. The choice had a ripple effect and the forces of hell will do anything they can to make bad matters worse.

Many believe in a real devil. The devil and his forces are devious and cunning. They will take any opportunity to infuse chaos and disease in people, young and old. Why bring up such a sober point? I've come to the place in my own spiritual journey that for me to stand, I need the help of God to fight things that I cannot see. Have you ever felt like you are being attacked on purpose? I remember a very volatile time in my marriage. Everything was getting twisted around. Some wonderful people came along side, prayed and talked with us to help us see that the devil was having a hay day. Have you sensed that something unseen is working hard to create chaos in your life and family? Call it what you will, but "hard-knock life" and "bad luck" just doesn't explain it enough for me. It is always easy to blame stuff on the devil. "The devil made me do it" has been an excuse for a long time, but Jesus did not react and totally dismiss the effect of the evil on the human condition. Jesus healed a lady who was crippled by spiritual power and who was bound by God's enemy for 18 long years (Luke 13). There was a physical attack by a spiritual being on this lady and Jesus set her free. I bring this up because there are times we need to consider that a spiritual component may exacerbate a physical problem. Contemplate what is going on within you and around you. If you feel that something that you cannot see continues to harass or attack, you may want to find some people that you feel spiritually safe with to help you fight back. (See Ephesians 6.10-17 for insight.)

My Reflections

_____

_____

_____

_____

_____

_____

_____

_____

_____

_____

_____

_____

_____

_____

_____

15. Kicked When You're Down

You may recall that Job was a really good guy and all of a sudden, his life shattered. He lost loved ones, his money and his health.

Job had three friends from out of town that came to visit and they sat with him for a week and said nothing. Not one word was spoken! Their gift was simply being present in the midst of so much suffering and loss. After a week, the silence was broken and the friends began to talk and then to preach. They exhorted Job to repent. They told Job that he had sinned. They blamed Job for questioning God. On and on the sermons went. It seems like everyone had an unsolicited opinion. Now, this sounds more like present-day life, doesn't it? Oh, that we had more friends who simply sat with us!

Sadly, most offer words of what would fix us. I'm sure they mean well, but we get kicked when we're down. When my brother was on the verge of dying, our family was told that if we had more faith, he would be healed. People told us that they understood what we were going through. Neither statement was true or helpful. There may be well-meaning people in life and they say some stupid, ignorant or wrong things. When we get kicked when we're down, what do we do?

Maybe we should begin to let it go. Forgive them for they don't know what they do (or say!). More than likely they are speaking out of their own anxieties. Sickness, uncertainty, and mystery make people nervous. Pat answers try to give explanation to the unknown. My friend who is battling cancer told me through her tears, "everyone is trying to boost me up and no one tries to understand." Today I just went and sat with her, and didn't say a word. What would you say to someone who just came and sat with you for a week?

What I Would Say to My Listening Friend

_____

_____

_____

_____

_____

_____

_____

_____

_____

_____

_____

_____

_____

_____

_____

_____

_____

_____

_____

16. More Than Reasons

One of my favorite biblical people who walked in open honesty is Job. The whole drama has such a modern ring to it: a faithful person of God has their world fall apart. Many a sincere person comes to God hurting with lots of questions. When I am hurting, I would really like to sit God down and get a good explanation for what is going on! I'd be so much more content if I got answers - reasons to why my situation is so painful and doesn't seem to be getting fixed. I typically believe that if I understand then all will be well. God thinks differently.

After Job and his friends "figured" God all out, God came to Job. Job wanted answers, but he got something else. God gave Job something better than reasons for pain. God gave a revelation of Himself. God asked Job questions for four chapters (Job 38-41) and the questions take Job to a place where he's in awe of the immensity of God. He had a revelation that God is so much bigger than he imagined and is up to stuff that he can't even fathom! God didn't explain Himself, but gave him perspective that the same God who controls the constellations and the crocodiles is still in control of our todays.

Chapter 42:1-6 says, "Then Job replied to the LORD: "I know that You can do all things; no plan of yours can be thwarted. You asked, 'Who is this that obscures my counsel without knowledge?' Surely I spoke of things I did not understand, things too wonderful for me to know. "You said, 'Listen now, and I will speak; I will question you, and you shall answer me.' My ears had heard of You but now my eyes have seen You. Therefore I despise myself and repent in dust and ashes."

Dear Lord, if we can't see the reasons, please let us see You. May we become so convinced of your sufficiency that our faith swells. May Your revelation make our need for answers fade.

My Reflections

_____

_____

_____

_____

_____

_____

_____

_____

_____

_____

_____

_____

_____

_____

_____

_____

_____

17. When, Not If

One of the things I have wrestled with is how to pray for healing. I've seen some people pray for healing in a way that seemed over the top. I've seen others who don't pray for healing because they believe that God doesn't heal. I have seen God's miraculous healing power, but I don't see it all the time. We're back at the mystery of God. So, if you really want to pray for yours or someone else's healing, how can you?

Sometimes people pray, "Dear God, if it is your will, please heal their disease." I used to pray that way a lot, but now I pray a bit differently, and it works better for me. Let's say we are praying for a person battling illness. We tend to think that the illness lasts forever, but forget that someday the illness will be gone.

So, when I pray, I'm looking at the illness as a temporary issue. "God, someday this illness will be gone and "Suzy" will live in wholeness for all eternity with you. Since this is her destiny, I pray that you would bring that eternal truth into this moment. Please back the future up to the present: on earth as in heaven. May heaven break into earth for Suzy right now."

This perspective takes the "if it is Your will" out of the equation. I know it is God's will that Suzy will live in wholeness, so now it becomes a question of when, not if. You may be dealing with yours or someone else's sickness. This is not the end. Someday it will be history! Lord, may someday be today!

"but we ourselves, who have the first fruits of the Spirit, groan inwardly as we wait eagerly for our adoption to sonship, the redemption of our bodies."
Romans 8.23

My Reflections

_____
_____
_____
_____
_____
_____
_____
_____
_____
_____
_____
_____
_____
_____
_____
_____
_____
_____
_____
_____
_____
_____

18. Wanda's Story

I started writing this book after several conversations with a fellow chaplain named Wanda. She was a woman of strong, but honest faith. I asked her to serve as my writing mentor because she knew better than most the power of God, faith, prayer and mystery. She had gone to a Bible School that strongly emphasized the healing of God, but her faith was deeply challenged when her granddaughter was tragically run over by a car and later died. Wanda was devastated that God didn't heal her granddaughter.

Over a long period of healing and struggle, she realized that her faith needed to be in God and not in faith. When she talked about it, I still could hear the pain and disappointment in her voice, but she knew that God wanted her to bring His love, presence, and mystery to hurting people. Many times she had to wrestle alone with her own pain, doubt, and confusion. She did not want anyone else to have to walk the valley floor alone. So she became a very good hospital chaplain. She didn't have to share her own story of pain, she knew that when she walked into the ICU, she was bringing God's love and healing to patients and families that were hurting, angry, and tired. She kept loving - she kept praying.

One time she prayed with a family and their loved one died. They were still all together for about 45 minutes after the doctor's pronouncement. Something in Wanda urged her to keep praying for the dead patient so she did. With a God-given fervor and intensity she prayed, and the patient began to breathe again and is still alive today. Wanda prayed and her granddaughter still died. Wanda prayed and the dead man woke up. That is the tension in which we live.

My Reflections

19. The Time is Not Yet- My Story

That Sunday night, we kids were asleep in bed all ready for another week of school. I heard a thud when my brother, Dan, slipped around the rail of the top bunk and fell to the carpet. When mom tried to get him back into bed, he acted strangely and complained about pain. The ambulance took him to the hospital and tests concluded a large clot was filling his seven-year-old skull. Doctors didn't think Daniel would live, but miraculously, he did. He remained in a coma for weeks.

All through the holiday season, people prayed and wept. Our church family stood with us night and day. When Daniel finally awoke, he was partially paralyzed with many medical issues. We prayed for more miracles and there were little improvements, but Dan's head injury spurred violent aggression. We kept praying to God for healing. For 17 years we prayed for Daniel and the Lord finally healed Daniel ...in heaven.

Sometimes God doesn't do what we want. We plead, we beg, we weep, we make promises, but sometimes God says, "No, not now." When God doesn't do what I asked, it is hard to swallow. I've blamed myself, "If only I had..." Now I realize that there are some things that simply won't make sense until the other side.

Have you ever seen cross-stitch? Looking at the back, you see strings and knots; it looks like one big mess. The pattern makes no sense at all. When you turn the pattern over to the front side, you see how all the knots and strings stitched together make beautiful artwork. There are some things in life that feel all knotted up, but will finally make sense when the pattern is stitched together into beautiful art and we gaze at it from the other side.

I still have questions about Daniel's accident and death. Our family experienced deep sorrow for years. God doesn't owe me an explanation. Someday I'll understand and you will too.

My Reflections

_____

_____

_____

_____

_____

_____

_____

_____

_____

_____

_____

_____

_____

_____

_____

20. The Time is Now! – Cindy's Story

A number of years ago, a young couple moved in across the street. We met them and exchanged pleasantries. Cindy was in her 20s and had attitude with a capital A. Cindy shared some her story with us: adopted ~ grew up in Reno ~ abusive mom ~ stepdad died ~ married with kids ~ female health issues.

Over time God allowed us to see Cindy take significant steps in her spiritual journey, and she helped us throw out the pastoral fluff and be more authentic. One day Cindy was pulling out of her driveway for a doctor appointment. We waved "hello" to her and she stopped. She shared that her ovaries (what was left of them) were giving lots of pain and problems. She was concerned that the doctor might want to remove the rest of her ovaries. Right in the middle of the street, we prayed for her and she went on her way. When she heard the results from the doctor, she bounced over to see us. God had healed her ovaries. They were whole, and the doctor could not explain it. About a year later, Cindy gave birth to a little boy...Toby is a gift from the Lord.

God does heal! It's okay to ask for a miracle. Many times as we hold hands around a bed, we pray for the healing touch of God. Sometimes we do see miracles, just like Cindy did. We see glimpses of God's will being done on earth as it is in heaven. Let's believe that God is still in the miracle working business. In Mark 5, we hear of a woman who had battled illness for 12 years. She had suffered much, but she came and touched the hem of Jesus' robe, and she felt in her body that she was healed. Jesus said to her, "Daughter, your faith has healed you. Go in peace and be freed from your suffering." Let's keep asking for miracles!

My Reflections

21. The Peace is There

My stomach was in knots and my life was spinning out of control. My to-do list was weeks behind schedule. I confided in a pastor-friend how heavy my heart felt. He told me that I needed a retreat. He offered to pay my way to go to a beachside cabin and spend time with God and just relax. I didn't have time to go retreat, but I went anyway.

I was at the cabin, feeling all fidgety, and decided to take a walk. The sun was setting as I walked along the beach. It felt like the first time in months that I had enough space to talk and listen to the Lord. Like a movie scene, porpoises were gliding in the water. Later, I saw two deer come out of a woodsy patch and prance along the shoreline as the water lapped quietly onto the beach. Suddenly, I had a "wow" moment. It seemed that God was saying to me, "David, the peace is already here. It is here everyday; you just need to create enough space to come to it."

I thought about my ministry, our new church start, my painting business, and my son in college...things that were clogging my mind with anxiousness. I would often frantically pray and ask God for peace. Now I realized that I needed to come to the peace. I needed to quiet my soul (Psalm 131.2) and listen to the water. I needed to look at the hues of the sunset. I needed to turn off my phone and turn on my quest for the still small voice of God. When I came to the peace, guess what happened? I found a quieted heart and a stillness to know God. So what can you do today to bring yourself to the peace? Reading some poetry or Scripture? Listening to music? Sitting by the pond? You may lack energy to do much, but how can you go and look for the peace that is there?

My Reflections

22. Beyond the Guessing Games

When something bad happens, a typical first thought is, "Uh oh, what did she do?" Job's friends came and preached to him that he must have done something to lose his health, his kids, and his fortune. At the end of story, God told Job's friends to have Job pray for them because they were all messed up. As a chaplain, I have shied far away from attaching blame for bad news or circumstances. Many times when something happens, the person didn't "do" anything. I hope that is a relief to you. Bad things really do happen to good people.

When bad things happen to me, I come to God. As I seek the Lord, I will ask how He is trying to get my attention. Sometimes a sin or a blind spot is pulling me further away from my connection with God. The Lord doesn't sit quietly by as our relationship unravels. The Scriptures tell us that some persons with habits of trite worship brought judgment on themselves - some actually got sick. (1 Corinthians 11.29f.) David, in Psalm 38, is allowing God to get his attention through suffering. David writes, "There is no soundness in my bones because of my sin." SOMETIMES God allows sickness because of sin. I even hate to write that because we tend to beat ourselves up with, "I must've done something to deserve this!" Stay with me for a moment, because this next point is crucial: David knew that God was allowing sickness to get his attention. I promise that God is not going to send sickness and then play cruel guessing games with us.

There is a wonderful promise in Philippians 3.12-15. The basic gist of the paragraph is this, "Run hard after God, let the past go and press on. Spiritually growing people do this. If you don't, God will make that clear to you and help you turn

44

around." It is God's job to let us know if we're not running well or if we've really blown it. If you are battling sickness, I bet God has your attention. Why not ask God if personal sin is contributing to this? If it is, then it is time to own up to it and turn from it. If God doesn't point anything out through prayer, Scripture, or people, then rest assured that personal sin is not the issue.

My Question for God

_____

_____

_____

_____

_____

_____

_____

_____

_____

_____

_____

_____

_____

_____

_____

_____

23. It's Your Turn Now

Years ago, a boy was afflicted with cerebral palsy. Something happened to his brain. He could think pretty well but he could not walk or talk. His body would not cooperate with his brain. He had gone through so much and his health problems were so pronounced that he hated himself and wanted to die. The only bright spot in his life was Mr. Rogers' Neighborhood on TV. He loved Mr. Rogers. His family found out that Mr. Rogers was coming to California and some people who cared deeply worked it out for the boy to meet Mr. Rogers.

There was so much anxiousness, fanfare, and stress that when the time came to meet Mr. Rogers, the boy started acting out. His mom took him to another room to calm him down. When they came back out, they were sure Mr. Rogers would have left, but he was still there. Mr. Rogers asked the boy if he could do something for him. He could not talk so he answered, "Yes" via a little computer screen. Mr. Rogers asked him to pray for him.

Later, an interviewer thought Mr. Rogers' action was brilliant because he was able to help the boy find hope and purpose. Rogers was surprised by this comment. He replied, ""Oh, heavens no! I didn't ask him for his prayers for him; I asked for me. I asked him because I think that anyone who has gone through challenges like that must be very close to God. I asked him because I wanted his intercession."

I share that story because it is time for you to acknowledge that with all you've been through, you see life, people, pain, and hope differently than most. It may be time for you to pray, write, encourage, call, email, or simply sit and listen with another. You know their plight is different from yours, but we have a shared humanity. You really have a gift and the choice is how will you share it.

My Reflections

_____

_____

_____

_____

_____

_____

_____

_____

_____

_____

_____

_____

_____

_____

_____

_____

24. The Hard Side of Faith

I hope the examples in this booklet have elevated your faith in a God who does miracles. I hope it has increased your honesty with a God who sometimes does not do miracles.

You may have heard of the list of people of faith from the Bible in Hebrews 11. It lists out so many biblical heroes who walked in faith and saw God show up. Noah, Abraham, and Moses are just a few of the great people of faith, but there is a section of Hebrews 11 that many skip over. I call it the hard part of faith. After reminding us of great people of faith, the writer says in 11:35-40,

"There were others who were tortured, refusing to be released so that they might gain an even better resurrection. Some faced jeers and flogging, and even chains and imprisonment. They were put to death by stoning; they were sawed in two; they were killed by the sword. They went about in sheepskins and goatskins, destitute, persecuted and mistreated— the world was not worthy of them. They wandered in deserts and mountains, living in caves and in holes in the ground. These were all commended for their faith, yet none of them received what had been promised, (emphasis added)

This is such a powerful paragraph! There were people who walked in faith, didn't see the promise on earth, but saw it in heaven. They see it now because their journey through the valley mysteriously connects to our faith and journey.

Sometimes, by faith, we get to see God break in and save the day, sometimes, by faith, we get to trust that God will break through even if He doesn't follow our clock or ways.

My Reflections

25. One Area You Control

Many hospital or hospice patients feel they have so little control. They have to follow what the doctors say. They'd better listen to the specialist. Nurses, techs, or even friends come into the room unannounced. Twenty-year old aides tell CEOs when bath time comes. Middle-aged women are required to wear ridiculous gowns in the hallway as they push around their IV bag. There seems to be no privacy, dignity, or control.

There is good news though. There is one area you do control. You decide to walk in bitterness or forgiveness. You can choose to let the doctor's lack of bedside manner ruin your day or decide that he may be better at practicing medicine than practicing friendship. You may choose to release the guilt of the tech that tried in vain to find a vein. You may choose to forgive the person who visits too often or not enough. You may choose to forgive the kitchen staff that gave you prunes instead of strawberry cake.

Forgiveness rarely happens by accident. I choose to forgive because God forgave me. God has forgiven me for more; I will forgive her for less. You've heard the statement to forgive seventy times seven (Matthew 18.22)? I used to pull out my calculator, but I've learned that it means to have a life of forgiveness. I may need to forgive someone a little bit every day for the one big thing they did. You have control. You must decide; no one will decide for you. Will you forgive?

> *"Dear God, I choose to forgive* _____ *for* _____
> *and* _____. *I let go of my bitterness. What they did
> really hurt me, but I place them in your hands."*

My Reflections

_____

_____

_____

_____

_____

_____

_____

_____

_____

_____

_____

_____

_____

_____

_____

_____

_____

_____

_____

26. More than Just Me

After nearly four years of pastoring my first church in a small farming community, everyone seemed to know that it was time for a change. I interviewed with a church in a nearby state and was well received by the church leaders. I was sure that I knew our next step. After a weekend of meetings and preaching, all of my optimism crumbled. A man in the church thought he should be the next pastor. When I came for my visit, he secretly led a coup to make sure I didn't get enough votes. So after I was voted down, my wife and I spent a lot of time consoling the heartbroken leaders who really wanted us to come. Deflated and embarrassed, I went back home and had to tell my current church that I wasn't going anywhere. They were politely gracious, but things were tense.

I wondered why God let me go through all of this. Why did God let some jerk ruin the whole opportunity? Why was I still stuck? What did I miss?

A couple of weeks later, I received a call from the Chairman of the Board's wife. It wasn't about our ministry, but about her marriage and family. The details are too complex, but their golden "Ken and Barbie" persona crumbled. My wife and I walked with this lady and her kids through the highly public and deeply painful breakup. I look back, now, and I see that God wanted us to stay in that farming town six months longer to shepherd hurting sheep.

It wasn't about me. Our pain and valley experiences are not all about us. There may be more than what we see. Could it be that we are in some valleys to walk with others who may be all alone, or who need an overflow of grace to touch them?

My Reflections

_____

_____

_____

_____

_____

_____

_____

_____

_____

_____

_____

_____

_____

_____

_____

_____

_____

_____

_____

_____

27. Just in Case

One of the saddest experiences in hospital chaplain ministry was with a family in strong denial. They were close and loved the Lord, but they were *not* dealing with the father's cancer, and were positive that God would heal him. They were so sure that God would heal him now, they would not even talk about possibility that He might not. As the dad grew worse, they kept praying and believing. I tried to minister to them, but they would put on the plastic smile and quickly excuse me. They worked so hard to say, do, and pray just the right thing, they never said goodbye to him. For them that wasn't faith.

I don't know your situation, but God does. As we've gone though this valley together, we've recalled how approaching God and circumstances with honesty and realism is a strong way to walk in faith. I hope you are able to have conversations with God and people, because frankly we do not know what is going to happen. Some people are so fearful to say the "right" words, they don't want to jinx themselves and appear to lack faith. Sadly, they don't honestly deal with their fears or uncertainties. They don't see that God may be saying "yes," "no" or maybe even, "It is time to come home to be with Me." It's hard to believe that God stands with us even when we don't understand or know what is coming next.

There is a wonderful Bible story of faith in Daniel chapter 3. You may recall the three men that refuse to bow down and worship the statue of their king. When they're confronted, they say, *"If we are thrown into the blazing furnace, the God we serve is able to deliver us from it, and he will deliver us from Your Majesty's hand. <u>But even if he does not</u>, we want you to know, Your Majesty, that we will not serve your gods or worship the image of gold you have set up."*

I love their faith because they are trusting God. They also know that God may be glorified in life or in death, so they tell the king that either way, they are walking in their faith.

My Reflections

_____

_____

_____

_____

_____

_____

_____

_____

_____

_____

_____

_____

_____

_____

_____

_____

_____

28. Peace and Pain

The story of my brother's head injury has affected my family deeply. During a particularly rough time, Daniel's treatment was not going well at all. The brain injury continued to spur erratic emotions and violent actions. Morale was low with Daniel, at the hospital, and at home. Mom went for a meeting with the therapist that ended awfully. It seemed like there was no hope or peace. To compound the chaos, it seemed like God's enemy had a megaphone to shout condemnation and accusation toward mom:

"Look at you. Victorious, aren't you? You mean you are still planning to speak at Christian Women's Club tomorrow? What are you going to tell them – how victorious you are in the battle? And how good God is? What's he done for you today?"

Mom went home feeling blasted and defeated. As she shared the war within, my dad said, "I'm learning that you can have pain in your heart and a settled peace in your soul at the same time, because the Shepherd is in control."

In the living room two hurting sheep came to the Good Shepherd and offered Him their pain once again. Where else could they go? The Shepherd was still in control. The next day mom went and spoke to a large group of women and shared her heart with them. They needed to hear that people could have a pain in the heart and a settled peace in the soul because the Shepherd is in control.

[If you'd like to read more detail, please see www.Amazon.com for Jane Bateman's book, "I Will Never" and the rest of the story.]

"Hear us, Shepherd of Israel, you who lead Joseph like a flock.
You who sit enthroned between the cherubim, shine forth...
Awaken your might; come and save us. Restore us, O God;
make your face shine on us, that we may be saved." Psalm 80

My Reflections

_____

_____

_____

_____

_____

_____

_____

_____

_____

_____

_____

_____

_____

_____

_____

_____

29. Can too! Cannot!

There are so many things that sickness or disease can do, isn't there? We feel poorly; we can't eat; we lose mobility. But there are some things that they cannot do. I'd never really thought about what they "can't" do until I walked into a little consult room on the cancer wing at the hospital where I worked. The room was nothing special but it held a powerful homemade cross-stitch framed on the wall. It read:

What Cancer Cannot Do: Cancer is so limited. It CANNOT "cripple love, shatter hope, corrode faith, destroy peace, kill friendship, suppress memories, silence courage, invade the soul, steal eternal life, conquer the Spirit." - (JLS 2000)

Isn't that beautiful? When I read that, I knew it was created by someone who knew well what cancer could and could not do. I felt like I was on holy ground. Sickness and pain and hurting tend to become preoccupying and all consuming, don't they? I've never had my pain say to me, "Oh, I can't conquer your Spirit." It just doesn't happen.

Today, let us speak hope and truth. Let us declare what your sickness can't do! Whatever that "it" is for you today, what can't it do? Where is it weak? Where is it anemic and powerless? It will scream, "Can too!" But today, we are settling on, "Cannot!"

"I know what it is to be in need, and I know what it is to have plenty. I have learned the secret of being content in any and every situation, whether well fed or hungry, whether living in plenty or in want. I can do all this through him who gives me strength." —St. Paul in Philippians 4.12

My Reflections

_____

_____

_____

_____

_____

_____

_____

_____

_____

_____

_____

_____

_____

_____

_____

_____

30. What Do You Really Want?

While reading the Bible, I've been struck by Jesus' questions.
One time he asked a blind man, "What do you want me to do
for you?" (Matthew 20.32). Another time he asked a disabled
man, "Do you want to get well?" (John 5.6) I wondered why
He asked those questions. What do you think? It seems
obvious from the outside that the blind want to see and the
lame want to walk. Why the questions?

Perhaps Jesus saw something in these folks. Maybe He wanted
them to stop and think about what they really wanted.
Sometimes we can be so stuck, so hurt, so sick, so
disappointed, that we begin to sing, "That's just the way it is,
some things never change…" We would never admit it, much
less bring it to a conscious level, but sometimes freedom and
healing are scary prospects. We've been reflecting in the valley
floor so long and now we know our way around quite well.
We see pain and hurt stare at us in the mirror and in one way
we hate it, but in a weird sort of way, it has become our closest
companion. It's hard to remember when things were different.

Someday soon, you may gaze up the mountainside and see the
sunlight flickering through the leaves. You may begin
imagining the warmth of the sun, the view from the top, the
cool breeze unhindered by the cloak of darkness. Picture for a
moment that Jesus is walking down the mountainside toward
you. Though you stand on the valley floor where the shadows
lurk and the sunlight is unwelcomed, you know that He sees all
of you with deep compassion in His eyes. Now imagine that
He kindly asks, "What do you want me to do for you?" What
will you say?

My Reflections

_____

_____

_____

_____

_____

_____

_____

_____

_____

_____

_____

_____

_____

_____

_____

_____

_____

_____

_____

_____

_____

ABOUT THE AUTHOR

David Bateman has been found wearing many different hats: husband ~ father ~ pastor ~ chaplain ~ house painter ~ schoolteacher ~ and Little League Coach.

He graduated with a Master's degree from Denver Seminary after receiving his Bachelor's degree through Moody Bible Institute, and Georgia State University. He started working on his Ph.D. but kept having more children.

David enjoys writing, teaching, hanging out watching a ball game, entrepreneurship, reading, biblical archeology, and power walking with his dog, Max. David and his family currently reside in Charleston, SC. He can be reached at DLBateman7@gmail.com .

40824422R00045

Made in the USA
Charleston, SC
17 April 2015